598.2   c.1

...in, Lynne

Peacocks

DATE			
NOV 2 5 '77	JUN 4 '82		
DEC 16 '77			
APR 1 4 '80			
APR 18 '80			
DEC 4 '80			
DEC 18 '80			
JAN 30 '8			
APR 27 '88			
OCT 2 0 '88			
APR 1 '89			
MAY 0 6 '13			

THE LIBRARY
CHILDREN'S LITERATURE COLLECTION
HUMBOLDT STATE UNIVERSITY
ARCATA, CALIFORNIA 95521

SUBJECT TO LATE FINE

© THE BAKER & TAYLOR CO.

PEACOCKS

LYNNE MARTIN

PEACOCKS

illustrated by Lydia Rosier
William Morrow and Company
New York 1975

Text copyright © 1975 by Lynne Martin
Illustrations copyright © 1975 by Lydia Rosier

All rights reserved. No part of this book may be reproduced or utilized in any form or by any means, electronic or mechanical, including photocopying, recording or by any information storage and retrieval system, without permission in writing from the Publisher. Inquiries should be addressed to William Morrow and Company, Inc., 105 Madison Ave., New York, N.Y. 10016.

Printed in the United States of America.
1 2 3 4 5 79 78 77 76 75

Library of Congress Cataloging in Publication Data

Martin, Lynne.
    Peacocks.

    SUMMARY: discusses the history, habits, and characteristics of the peacock.
        1. Peafowl–Juvenile literature. [1.Peafowl]
I. Rosier, Lydia, ill. II. Title.
QL696.G27M37   598.6'1   74-34179
ISBN 0-688-22032-0
ISBN 0-688-32032-5 lib. bdg.

    598.2
    C.1

THE LIBRARY
CHILDREN'S LITERATURE COLLECTION
HUMBOLDT STATE UNIVERSITY
ARCATA, CALIFORNIA 95521

To Betty and Ed Parsons

By the Same Author
The Orchid Family

CONTENTS

The Peacock Family   9

Plumage   30

Mating and Raising Young   42

Living Habits   54

Over the Ages   67

On Display   82

Index   95

THE PEACOCK FAMILY

The peacock is famous for his fancy feathers, proud bearing, and stately strut. He is a handsome bird in any pose. But when the peacock lifts his long train of feathers and spreads it into a fan adorned with the glittering eyes of gold and green, purple and blue, then his true glory is revealed.

The dazzling show begins with a soft, rustling sound like that of a breeze whispering through a bamboo forest. Slowly the three-foot plumes float upward, followed by a second row of even longer, stiffer plumes, until the enormous feathery fan spans nine feet in width. As it sways high, the fan of feathers and fringe shoots off sparks of metallic luster. Bracing the fan and holding it aloft is the peacock's true tail, a plain,

ordinary, brown tail like that of any other bird.

During the display, which can last only seconds or for longer then an hour, the peacock dances. The bird takes a step or two at a time, turning just a bit to the right, then to the left on his heavy white legs.

The full spectacle of a peacock displaying his plumes is a sight no one ever forgets. In the magnificence of its color and form and the drama of its surprise, the display is not matched by any other bird. No wonder then that some people call the peacock the king of birds. Appropriately an erect crest of gold-tipped feathers crowns the delicate head.

The smaller peahen also bears this fan-shaped head crest but has no ornamental train and less brilliant plumage. As among so many other birds, the male peacock is the more brightly colored of the sexes. Peahens, like most female birds, are plain by comparison and more protectively marked.

The correct zoological name of both male and

female of this species is peafowl. However, the bird's scientific generic name, *Pavo,* is Latin for *peacock,* which is what most people call this beautiful creature.

Peacocks are glorified chickens, according to the scientists who classify all members of the bird world by their structure and habits. Like their humble relatives in the barnyard, peacocks are "gallinaceous" birds, scratchers of the ground.

They belong to the same family as the pheasants, which includes Old World quails and partridges, as well as the jungle fowl. This enormous worldwide family—called Phasianidae

rooster and hen

pheasant

—contains some of the most popular game birds and many other birds noted for their beauty. It also has contributed the domestic chicken to the dinner tables of mankind.

All true pheasants are noted for their long, ornate, arched tails and fairly long scaled legs, usually spurred. Chickens and their ancestors, a species of wild jungle fowl, differ from other pheasants in that they have a comb and wattles and their tail is more arched and curved. What distinguishes the peacock from every other member of the Phasianidae is the wonderfully elongated train with the mysterious eyes.

Wild peafowl have been admired since their discovery in the Far East tens of centuries ago. They are, with few exceptions, good-natured toward man as well as other birds. In captivity, the hardy birds thrive on a simple diet and require minimum care and shelter. So their fame spread through the years as tame specimens were brought to all parts of the world to live in all kinds of climates. The large size and gorgeous plumage of the adult peacock make it one of the most ornamental and popular birds for display in zoological gardens, city parks, country estates, home gardens and aviaries to this day.

There are two true species of wild peafowl: the Indian blue peafowl — *Pavo cristatus* — and the Javan green peafowl — *Pavo muticus*. Rich jewels in the feathered kingdom, one sparkles like a sapphire, the other glows like an emerald.

In their native Asiatic regions peafowl generally live in open, low, hot country, seldom ven-

turing above elevations of 3000 feet. They shun the wide-open plains as well as the deep unbroken forests, preferring parklike land with scattered trees or scrub. Peafowl frequent riverbanks and forest clearings as long as the birds can find sufficient cover in the form of trees, shrubs, or long grass.

Common Indian peafowl, as the Indian blue peafowl is sometimes called, is better known, more abundant, and ranges over a wider area than the Javan peafowl. It is the national bird of India. *Pavo cristatus* inhabits large areas of India from the foothills of the Himalayan Mountains south to the island of Ceylon. It is naturally accustomed to the tropical heat of this territory; nevertheless, it has the ability to endure without discomfort temperatures well below zero. This adaptability has enabled the Indian blue peafowl to live in most countries of the world, and it is the bird most often seen in captivity.

In Hindu lands where Indian peafowl are held sacred, they are respected and never molested. They become tame and live around human settlements, visiting towns, villages, and temples where people feed them. In the vicinity of shrines in the Indian hills, they flock together from the nearby forests in great numbers. Suddenly the sky may come alive with the brilliant birds, several hundred winging over narrow

18

valleys, scores rising above the formation, flying over the backs of others and skimming the tops of low trees.

Sometimes they raid the cultivated fields of a farmer and have to be chased away. Boys sit in tree shelters and pull cords attached to slender poles, which support empty kerosene tins and scarecrows. Should peafowl or other animal marauders come to eat the grain, the boys jerk

the cords and hopefully frighten off the culprits
by the jangling cans at night and the wriggling
scarecrows during the day. A peafowl's taste for
buds and flowers also makes the bird unwelcome
in small gardens.

When peafowl have been persecuted for their flesh or feathers, they prove to be extremely shy. The Javan green peacock is a wilder and warier bird than the blue peacock, probably because it was not protected by religious beliefs in its habitat. Living east of India, *Pavo muticus* ranges from Burma in the north, southward to Thailand, Vietnam, the Malay Peninsula, and Java. For some curious reason the birds are not found on the nearby islands of Borneo and Sumatra.

Javan green peacock

The Javan peafowl is a more delicate species than the Indian and cannot endure cold winters. Even so, it does well in captivity if the less hardy bird is sheltered in freezing weather. As adults, Javan peacocks are bad tempered and quarrelsome; males often battle each other savagely. Occasionally they attack the peahens too, and several of them cannot be kept together in the same park or pen. When they become aggressive toward human beings, which happens now and then, the birds are a real menace because of their sharp leg spurs.

Despite these drawbacks, many people consider the slimmer green peacock to be the most beautiful of all birds, even more splendid than his Indian relative. Not only does this aristocrat among peacocks parade with a more erect posture, he seems more graceful. He struts on considerably longer legs, and his neck is longer and slimmer too.

The voice of the Javan peacock differs considerably from the disagreeable screech of the Indian bird. In fact, the word *muticus* in his scientific name means *silent* in Latin, which he does not entirely deserve. Still, his call is less harsh.

The distinguishing word *cristatus* in the scientific name of the Indian peacock means *crested* in Latin. Nevertheless, male and female birds in both species are crested.

The following list shows other differences between the two species of peacocks:

Peafowl have brown eyes and stout, hooked bills. Their bone-white, unfeathered legs have spurs and four widespread toes. The birds are noted for their ugly feet, but the large, strong toes are perfectly adapted for scratching in the earth for food. A peacock is about as large as a turkey, the average weight being ten pounds. With his train trailed behind him, a peacock measures from six to eight feet in length, including four to six feet of glorious train feathers.

Besides the typical Indian peafowl, there are three other well-known color phases of the spe-

white peacock

cies in captivity. Apparently there are no wild birds of these types.

One of the most frequently admired is the white peacock, pure white from crest to toes, but with brown eyes. It is an albino variety lacking color pigments, selectively bred from "sports," or mutations, which occur when peafowl breed in zoos or wherever they are raised. When a peacock is pure white, head, body, and train, it is a very striking object, especially if the snowy plumage is raised. Each white eye structure is clearly visible on the many lacy plumes. Such a bird seems like the ghost of a real peacock.

Another variety, the pied peacock, results when white and Indian blue peafowl are bred. Usually this hybrid bird inherits the color and pattern of the Indian peafowl's body and train, with white wings and large, regular white markings replacing the normal colors here and there.

The black-winged peafowl (called a black-shouldered peafowl by some) is a recognized mutation of the Indian peafowl, with wings of shining iridescent black contrasting with an even deeper shade of blue on the neck and breast. Many consider this variety even more beautiful than the parent form.

Hybrids are common among green and blue peafowl in captivity, since the two crossbreed freely. The offspring are entirely fertile, and the

black-winged peacock

handsome adult birds are as hardy and good-tempered as pure Indian peafowl.

For a long time naturalists believed that all the typical pheasants were natives of southern Asia. In 1936, however, Dr. James P. Chapin, an authority on the birds of the Congo, startled the scientific world by describing an African species. From then on the two species in the genus *Pavo* had a near relative in a distant land. It was named *Afropavo congensis,* African peacock from

Congo peafowl

the Congo, or Congo peacock, as the name is usually translated.

Despite the lack of any train or of eyespots in

the plumage, the bird's peacock relationship is evident in its habits and appearance. The male is largely gleaming black with bronze-green-purple-blue metallic highlights; the female is a soft brown below and green on the back with dark markings. Both sexes have an upstanding crest. The female's is buff colored; the male's is black and has a tuft of stiff white bristles in front of it. The unfeathered skin of the face is a blue-gray color.

From their roosts in tall trees in the equatorial forest at night, Congo peafowl fill the air with their shrill cries to each other. In imitation of the birds' call, the Babali of Africa has given the bird the name *ngowe.* The mounting uproar continues as the birds call and answer back and forth perhaps thirty times without letup. This performance betrays them to hunters, although they are protected by law. In 1949, a New York Zoological Society expedition brought six males and one female to the Bronx Zoo, the first specimens exhibited alive.

PLUMAGE

When the peacock spreads his train, a hundred
eyes sparkle in the sunlight, splashed in a symmetrical pattern over the 200 feathers that make
up the fan. The most common error is to regard
the eyed feathers as the tail or wing feathers.
Upper tail coverts and lower back feathers form
the train, and they cover the real tail quills.

The wheel of long, flexible plumes is erected,
backed, and steadied by twenty plain but stiff
tail feathers, which are thrust up by strong
muscles under the skin of the rump. Now the
peacock's tail stands up at a right angle to his
back. The upper tail coverts are forced into an
upright position. They, in turn, raise the feathers
of the upper back, which form a metallic green
shield. Some tail coverts extend out horizontally,

even downward, trailing on the ground. Meantime, the bird's half-spread wings are hidden behind the fan.

Then the peacock braces itself and gives a long quivering shudder to spread the train and settle the plumes in the new fan position. This

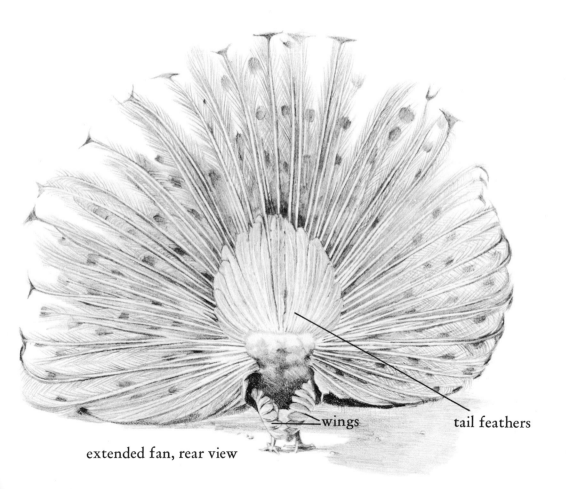

wings

tail feathers

extended fan, rear view

feat accomplished, the bird swaggers slowly to and fro. Certainly the courting peacock displays his train as part of a mating dance to attract peahens. But he is just as likely to parade and turn and bow before human admirers or even his own reflection on the side of a shiny car parked at the zoo.

The display also seems to provide an outlet for a number of emotions. Peacocks, before they begin to battle a peacock competitor, will often erect their trains and circle one another. Hens erect their tails and rush forward at any enemy that threatens their brood of chicks. The chicks themselves imitate the fighting tactics of their elders when only a few weeks old.

No one, except perhaps the peacock, knows if he is really proud of his great beauty, though the expression, "proud as a peacock" usually labels someone who is vain. Some scientists say that the peacock struts in his measured way simply to keep his balance beneath the swaying plumage. A high wind does indeed present a real threat to

his dignity, for then the bird battles valiantly to
keep his big train up high while he tries to stay
upright.

When the train is fanned out, it can prove a
nuisance in another way: the peacock cannot see
what is going on behind him. Thus, a peck on his

exposed rump from any rival bird can put a hasty end to the peacock's performance.

The long train, when not displayed, is compactly folded back. It causes little hindrance to the bird either running through grass or when it takes off in flight with the strong, rounded wings.

Early-morning dew burdens the train feathers and so does rain. However, peacocks habitually remain on their high tree roosts until the moisture evaporates. Even a cloak of snow is only temporarily troublesome for the Indian peafowl, which withstand severe winters outdoors at the Bronx Zoo.

Peacocks have the same three main types of feathers found in the plumage of the average bird. The straight, stiff, tightly meshed flight feathers of the wings and tail enable the bird to fly. Smaller, softer, often curved contour feathers cover the body and give the bird its typical smooth and streamlined look. Small, loose, fluffy down feathers make up the first plumage of young birds and are also present beneath the contour feathers next to the skin of adult birds.

The many ornamental plumes of the train, however, do not even vaguely resemble feathers as we know them, so different are they in shape, size, texture, and especially color.

Think of a typical flight feather with its simple parts: (1) The smooth, hollow "quill" is the base and extends into (2) the central part of the feather called the "shaft," which supports (3) rows of branched "barbs," which hook together and form the feather "vane." Imagine the quill and shaft as the trunk of a tree; the barbs grow out like branches, and "barbules," which hook one barb to the next, are like little twigs on each barb. The barbs mesh tightly and form a firm, flat surface.

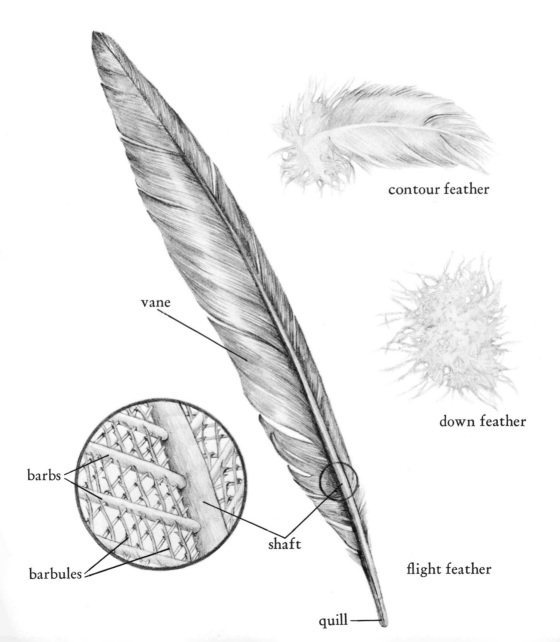

vane

contour feather

down feather

barbs

barbules

shaft

flight feather

quill

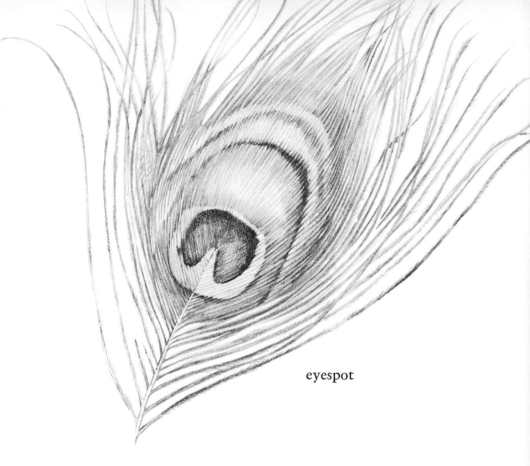

eyespot

The disintegrated barbs on a peacock's train feather are long and flexible, and only the eyespot near the tip of the plume is flat and tightly meshed. Under a microscope an eyespot looks like a closely woven mat.

Charles Darwin, the famous scientist, thought the peacock eye feather was one of the most beautiful objects in nature. Each eyespot, or "ocellus," is composed of a deep blue patch surrounded by two broad rings of brilliant turquoise blue and bronzy brown and two narrow ones of golden green and bronzy lilac. Tufts of bronze-green barbs fringe the outer edge.

The multicolored design of the great round eyes, or "ocelli," seem to glow with a hundred iridescent colors. Yet the true color of the substance that makes up these feathers is brown.

Structurally peacock feathers are a complex of horny layers called "keratin." They consist of the same material that makes the horn of certain animals and the skin, hair, and fingernails of human beings. The outermost keratin layer is much thinner than the page on which these words appear, but it, in turn, consists of numerous transparent layers that are one ten-thousandth of an inch thick, with grooves and ridges that catch and scatter the light like a splintered rainbow.

The submicroscopic horny layers are thickly

packed with many-sided cells. Each cell is peppered with tiny granules of a dark brown pigment called "melanin" (from *melan,* which is the Greek word for *black*). Pigments are similar to coloring substances such as paints or dyes; the color of our skin, the green color in leaves, and the color of flowers are due to the presence of pigment cells. The iridescent colors so commonly observed in peacock feathers are created by the dense and precise arrangement of melanin particles within the many thin layers of horn, which reflect light from both the top and bottom surfaces. Just as light is reflected in a soap bubble, the rainbow colors change by the split second, depending on the angle of light and the angle of observation.

The moment arrives once a year in every adult peafowl's lifetime when the feathers are shed to make room for new growth. The process, called "molting," occurs in an orderly fashion lasting several weeks. The bird can still fly because flight feathers from the wings and tail are shed and replaced rapidly and in symmetrical pairs.

As the beautiful ocellated train feathers fall one by one, new plumes begin to develop for each molted one. By late summer the molt is complete, but during the process the peacock presents a rather ragged appearance. Seven months pass before the peacock has a totally new set of fancy feathers to display as another spring and another season for courtship begins.

peacock during molting

MATING AND
RAISING YOUNG

How can such elegant creatures make such ugly sounds? No peacock ever uttered the musical tones we associate with many birds. Instead, his call is considered a sad squawk by some, an unearthly scream or a rusty screech by others. A peacock's cry can be heard from a distance of two miles. No wonder then that indignant taxpayers have called the National Zoo in Washington, D.C., to demand that they stop the peacocks' continuous racket so that they can get some sleep. Their raucous and almost human calls do not make peacocks popular in urban areas that have been zoned as residential districts.

The bird takes as much pleasure in calling as it does in showing off its train. Little excuse is needed. A peal of thunder, the noise of a top-

pling tree branch, or a car backfiring rouses every bird within hearing distance to join in an unmelodic chorus.

Peacock vocalizations indicate such things as alarm, threat, and courtship, much the same as those of other birds. On being suddenly frightened, peafowl sound a loud *kok-kok-kok-kok*. The peahen's call is not so loud, but equally shrill. Peachicks have a soft chirp, and when the mother is content or chides the chicks, the calls have no harshness.

Never are peacocks noisier than during the breeding season. This season varies, according to the latitude of the peafowl's habitat, anywhere from early spring to late summer. A month or more after peacocks have attained their full "nuptial," or breeding, plumage, they begin calling regularly.

courtship display

By his calls and aggressive behavior, the peacock establishes his territory. He will instinctively attach himself to a piece of territory with invisible boundaries and mercilessly attack anything that threatens his domain. Battles between peacocks are neither frequent nor very fierce. Occasionally rivals rush toward each other with

loud cries of outrage. A few such warnings send the intruder off to find a place of his own to which he can attract a female, a place that will also provide protection and sufficient food for a growing family.

Peafowl are polygamous in breeding habits; each peacock is paired to two or more mates during the courtship season. Usually one peacock secures a harem of three to five hens. The peacock's courtship display is a form of animal language. It involves a series of signals that enable males and females to recognize each other as members of the same species. This instinctive behavior also helps intensify the mating drive.

The mating ritual begins when the peacock erects his splendid curve of train feathers. The bird takes a few paces, to the left, to the right, and bows toward the hen of his choice. Suddenly he rushes forward, and with a great quiver of his whole body the peacock clatters his fan quills together. The sound is a cross between that made by a baby's rattle and the soft, rustling sound of rain pattering on dry leaves. The peacock gives an abrupt screech; then slowly he turns around in front of the peahen. At other times the peacock approaches the hen by pacing backward. At the last moment he turns toward her. In this way he emphasizes the contrast between the dull brown shades of his rear with the fan of feathers that vibrates split-second changes of flashing colors.

Is she impressed? How does the peahen react to the colors, motions, and sounds of the courting peacock? The peahen may ignore him. Casually she pretends to peck at seeds on the ground. This indifferent attitude is typical of how most female birds act toward courting males. She spurs him to greater efforts. The most persistent, not necessarily the most handsome, peacock often attracts a number of females as the first step in the reproductive cycle. In time, the females are influenced by the peacock's colors, the quill music, and the harsh scream, and mating will take place throughout the breeding season.

Peacocks have little to do with building a nest or with the rearing of the young birds. For nesting places the peahens prefer tall grass or a clump of shrubs in fairly open places, rather than the dense cover found in deep forest. No nest is made on the ground; only a shallow hollow is scratched out and the eggs are deposited on the bare earth over a period of a week or more. Five to eight eggs form the normal clutch, or set. The large spotless eggs measure two inches by three inches. The shells are thick and glossy white or cream colored. If the first clutch is destroyed, or if some of the eggs are taken away (as might be the case in a zoo or aviary, for example) the peahens renest, often repeatedly.

If several peahens make their nest together, they take turns sitting on the eggs to keep them warm. During the breeding season incubating birds develop a brood patch, which is a thin-feathered area with a higher-than-normal skin temperature. When a peahen settles upon the nest, she parts the breast feathers so that they surround the eggs. Thus, the heat of the body, via the brood patch, is transferred directly to the eggs. Peahens incubate their eggs with attentive periods at the nest and inattentive periods away. The incubation period is usually twenty-eight days.

Peachicks are equipped with an egg tooth, a tiny protruding horn on the tip of the upper beak. It is used to open the shell and disappears soon after hatching. The chick kicks itself free of the cracked shell after several hours or more.

Young birds are commonly divided into two types. The first are called "altricial." They are birds like the robin, which are born naked in a helpless condition and dependent on parental care. The second are called "precocial." They are born with eyes open, have a covering of down feathers, can move right away, and are only

peachick

partly or not at all dependent on the parents. Peachicks, like other gallinaceous birds in the pheasant family, are fully covered with natal down feathers and scamper from the nest soon after hatching. As precocial types, the young birds flutter to a low branch and perch when only a week old.

Peahens continue to brood or cover their young to keep them warm at night and at intervals during the day, especially during spells of bad weather. The peahen is an excellent mother, and the chicks have the habit of taking shelter under her tail. Young birds, even though the species is mainly seed-eating, are fed animal food at first, especially grubs and other insects. Soon the chicks forage for themselves after accompanying their mother on their first explorations.

The down that peachicks are born with is soon molted. The incoming plumage first appears as stiff quills, which push the down outward. These quills gradually rupture and unfold their feathers. The chicks and first-year young resemble the peahen in their modest brown color. The males show more neck color, have a spotted back, a longer crest, and are larger than hen chicks.

While peahens lay many eggs the first year, the peacock does not become adult and complete his plumage until the third year. The length of the train, however, increases until the fifth or sixth year of his life.

week-old chicks

LIVING HABITS

Peacocks settle down after the noisy exhibition and productive activity of courtship and breeding. They assemble in small groups with a few females and young during the late spring and summer. Later, in the postnesting season, peafowl gather in large flocks. The birds that were segregated on private territories during the breeding season become neighborly again, indicating that peafowl are fundamentally sociable in nature.

Before sunrise, the birds descend from the tall trees where they roost at night. With a flutter of wings, the peacock leads and the hens follow in a long, graceful glide to the ground, ending in rapid wingbeats or sometimes an undignified half tumble if they encounter a branch or bush before they reach the ground.

Food and drink are the first order of the day. The two main feeding periods occur in the morning and in late afternoon. Some peafowl wander to a riverbank to drink deeply, dipping into the water, then raising their heads in order to swallow. Others pick here and there at the water's edge among the reeds and later search the clearings and forest borders for grasses, grains, buds

and flowers, leaves, vegetables, berries and other fruits. They feed on small-sized animal life too: insects, molluscs, lizards, frogs, and snakes.

Peafowl always feed on the ground. They scratch vigorously with their strong-clawed toes, unearthing grubs and worms, and dig into the hard nesting mounds of termites. The strong hooked bill is used to scrape the sunbaked earth.

External nares, or nostrils, open into the base of the horny beak, but the sense of smell is of little importance to peafowl. Peafowl, of course, have no teeth and do not chew food; instead,

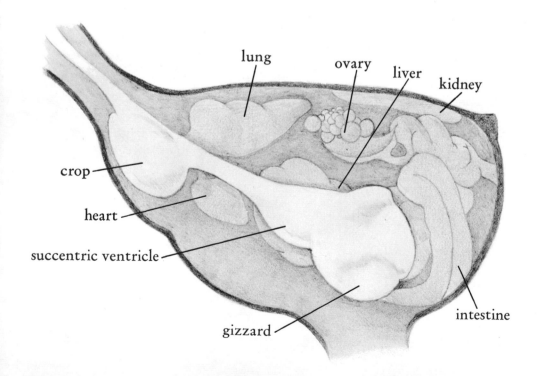

they bolt it quickly for storage in the crop, a pouched enlargement of the digestive tube. This organ enables birds to take in large quantities of food at a faster rate than their small stomach can digest it. Thus, gallinaceous birds gobble up a cropful of grain at a particular feeding time and then pass on the stored items a few at a time to be digested while resting or roosting. The stomach of a peafowl is divided into two portions. The smaller front compartment secretes gastric fluids that moisten the food before it passes on to the thick, muscular gizzard, or second part. Grain-eating birds have the most powerful gizzards for crushing hard pieces such as seeds, often with the aid of sand or small pebbles swallowed by the bird.

Peafowl are fairly sedentary birds. They rarely move rapidly, although they are capable of swift, short flights. Nor do they migrate seasonally for long distances like many bird species. If the food and drinking places in a region are plentiful, their visits are as regular as their evening return to a favorite roost. As the heat of the day increases, many of the flock mount to a favorite low, bare branch shaded by overhead foliage. Some birds sleep at this time; others preen their plumage.

The birds spend a lot of time caring for their feathered bodies. Whenever the feathers get ruffled, dirty, or wet, the bird carefully smooths and straightens out each feather with its beak. The bird's long neck helps it to reach all parts of its body. Preening is one of the most important chores of the bird's daily routine, for its life may depend on the feathers functioning properly. Smooth muscles and elastic fibers in the skin permit the bird to fluff the feathers at will, raising them away from the skin for cleaning and rearranging.

You will never see peafowl enter the water to bathe the way a robin likes to duck and frolic in a birdbath or puddle. No gallinaceous bird water bathes.

When preening, peafowl rub their beak over an oil gland located immediately in front of their

tail. The oil they spread through their feathers serves as a water repellent and provides better insulation against heat and cold. Scientists also think the oil helps prevent a bone disease known as rickets. The oil may be absorbed by the skin as vitamin D when activated by the sun's rays, or the bird may swallow oily feather particles in the act of preening.

Peafowl may spend an hour a day oiling their feathers and another hour dust bathing. The main purpose of the dust baths is to absorb excess amounts of oil, which attract annoying parasites. The parasites feed on oils and not directly on the bird. Thus, dusting defeats parasites since it limits their food supply. Several birds may take a dust bath together. They hollow out cavities in dry earth. Half hidden in the hollow, they flip clouds of dust over their bodies with great sweeps of one wing. After distributing the dust, the birds rise, shake themselves, and retreat to the shade of a nearby bush where they continue the violent shakings and resume preening.

With the same feather-fluffing action the peafowl uses to preen its feathers, the bird provides its own built-in heating system when it lives in cold climates. Feathers are the most efficient type of insulation known. As warm-blooded creatures birds maintain extremely high body temperatures, commonly 104 to 112 degrees, even in subzero weather. The peafowl's feathers are full of dead air spaces, especially when fluffed out. Fluffing out the feathers increases the insulation by trapping more air between the feathery layers, reducing heat loss to a minimum.

Sleeping birds commonly tuck their bill in their feathers in cold weather. In this way they reduce internal heat loss when breathing. Their breathing rate and general body metabolism are lowered as well.

In general, larger birds like peafowl withstand extremes of cold better than small ones. Even the bird's feet and legs don't feel the cold much since they contain no fleshy muscles, only tough tendons with a limited nerve supply and sluggish circulation.

And how does a peacock cool off in warm weather? It can get very hot in the peafowl's natural habitat, yet the birds walk about casually under a blazing sun with the thermometer at 147 degrees Fahrenheit. The bird simply reverses the action of ruffling its feathers and holds them close to the body, which allows some escape of body heat. A bird gaping with open mouth in hot weather is not panting for breath. Since the peafowl has no sweat glands, it disperses heat and moisture by gulping in air and sending it through the lungs and out the wide-open mouth, along with excess body heat.

It is fortunate for peafowl that the almost glandless body is practically free of odor. Predators on the hunt find that peafowl are difficult to scent. The birds live in the same habitat as tigers, leopards, and civets, as well as smaller jackals and martens. Large hawks are also a menace.

A peacock is highly visible because of its size and colorful plumage. Even so it is not a skulking bird that tries to hide from its enemies. In

tiger

spite of the handicap of feathers, it can defend itself with its sharp spurs against the smaller car-
nivorous animals and birds of prey. It prefers,
however, to escape danger, which it detects with
its keen sense of sight and hearing, by means of
flight or a swift run for cover. When feeding in
open places, the birds continually glance upward
and cock their head from side to side to spot any
danger on the ground.

Peafowl ears have no outer chambers for hearing like ours. Instead, the external ear openings are covered by a special group of feathers, the "auriculars," which are delicately and loosely constructed. They can actually be lifted slightly when a peacock is listening intently.

Around sunset, peafowl start coming in from all directions to their favorite place to spend the night. The last ones arrive just before dark. They almost always choose to roost among the branches of high isolated trees with slick branchless lower trunks. Animals that hunt by night cannot climb the great smooth-barked trunks of these trees. Before takeoff from the ground, the bird first looks in all directions and listens intently. Then, sometimes on a run, the peacock beats heavily and rapidly with his wings and rises at a sharp angle to a low tree, then a higher tree, and finally the lofty perch where he will spend the night. The hens follow at intervals, flying more easily. They settle down close together, all facing one way. If a strong wind is blowing, the birds roost facing into it.

There is a good deal of calling back and forth as they first congregate. The harsh resounding *he'-on* or *h-o-ha* cries of the peacock are produced in a special structure called the "syrinx," or voice box. It lies at the lower end of the long, flexible, partially looped windpipe, or "trachea." Air expelled from the lungs passes between and vibrates the membranes of the syrinx chamber, whose tension is under delicate muscular control. Then up and out of the windpipe trumpet the raucous sounds for which peacocks are famous. In a little while, after some restlessness, the peafowl quiet down and the quick tropical night closes in.

OVER THE AGES

The peacock is the oldest as well as the showiest of ornamental birds known to man.

Astonished by its beauty, men have worshiped the peacock in their poems, fables, religions, and art over the ages of recorded history. Royal fortunes have been lavished for its acquisition and upkeep in elaborate gardens. The ancient Greek naturalist Aristotle once commented, however, "The peacock is a pestilent thing in gardens, doing a world of mischief. It throws down the roof tiles and plucks off the thatch of houses." In earlier times, at least some people thought the peacock had "the feathers of an angel, but the voice of a devil and the innards of a thief."

Long before his discovery by the Western world, the peacock was said to be sacred to the gods and he was allowed to reign undisturbed among the flowers and trees in the gardens of Indian princes. Gradually the territory of the peacock spread.

The Phoenicians, about 1000 B.C., were the first to bring the birds over land and sea to adorn royal gardens of Egyptian pharaohs. Even King Solomon, the Bible tells us, dispatched his mighty ships to the Orient every three years and replenished his supplies of "gold and silver, ivory . . . and peacocks."

When Alexander the Great embarked on an expedition to India, he and his soldiers returned to ancient Greece with the noble birds. Impressed by their beauty, Alexander issued an order to prevent any killing of peafowl, with the severest penalties for violators. People came from neighboring towns and assembled in crowds to see the rare birds in the city of Athens.

Until the Middle Ages, it was the costliest bird in Europe. Only kings and nobles could afford it, and they would pay a fortune for a breed-

ing pair. At one time Athenians paid nearly ten thousand drachmae for a peacock, compared to the value of a domestic rooster, which cost only five drachmae. A breeding pair was worth the high price, since peafowl breed easily and the chicks could be sold for high sums or kept for their desirable feathers. The train feathers with their glittering eyes were valuable enough to be sold one by one.

The ancients explained how the peacock came to have eyes on its train in the famous myth about the goddess Juno. On Mount Olympus a peacock was Juno's constant companion while down below the birds were free to roam her temples. Juno, who had always been suspicious of her wayward husband Jupiter, was especially jealous of a young nymph named Io. In an effort to avoid trouble with his wife, Jupiter transformed Io into a calf in the hope of spending more time with her in this new disguise. Juno discovered his trickery and dispatched the giant Argus, who had a hundred eyes, to spy on her calf-rival. However, Jupiter found out about her plan, and he ordered Mercury to slay this guard who could see in all directions and who never slept. Mercury accomplished his mission by playing hypnotic music on his pipes. Slowly, one by one, Argus's hundred eyes closed, whereupon Mercury chopped off his head. Heartbroken over this turn of events, Juno decreed that the hundred eyes of Argus be transferred to the train of her favorite bird, the peacock.

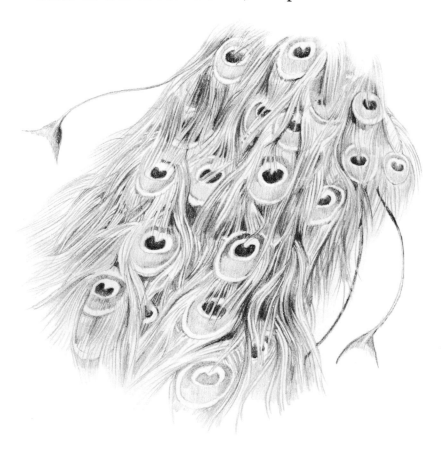

In later years, the Romans apparently were more fond of feasting than gazing on beautiful birds, and they made peafowl part of their famous banquets. Vitellius, a Roman emperor, treated his guests to platters of peacock tongues and brains, which were considered special delicacies. Such a hard, gristly morsel as a bird's tongue, however, could hardly have been more satisfying for supper than the scales on the legs of the bird.

English barons of the Middle Ages presented evidence of their wealth by serving roast peacock at their banquets. The bird was surrounded by prunes, which were then very rare. Fancier fare was yet to come as medieval cooks tried to outdo each other. One fourteenth century cook had a peacock skinned, stuffed, and roasted. Then the skin, with every feather in place, was draped around the roast fowl, the long train trailing gracefully behind. The finishing touch? A brandy-soaked feather was put in the peacock's bill, set aflame, and the proud cook carried his work of art into

the dining hall on a gigantic platter. Another
cook was even more inventive. Into one peacock
ready for roasting, he inserted a cleaned and
boned goose, into it, a plump hen; then a partridge, a quail, and finally a lark were all stuffed

one inside the other. When the roasted master-piece was carved, each steaming slice included the meat of six different birds.

During this era in France, the Vow of the Peacock was a solemn ritual pronounced at table over a platter of peacock roasted and dressed in its feathers. Before carving the bird, each knight extended his hand over it and pledged to accomplish some mighty deed by saying, "I vow to God, to the Virgin Saint, to the Ladies, and to the Peacock." He then was served a slice of peacock. Failure to do whatever he promised was

deemed a black mark against his name. In those days, the peacock's flesh was considered incorruptible, and supposedly this sterling quality would pass onto anyone who dined on peacock.

Peacock plumes were widely used to decorate household screens, mats, fans, and various types of headgear in many lands. (Not long ago, the tomb of a Viking warrior was discovered in Norway, and along with the Norseman's armor and weapons a packet of peacock feathers was found. Although the plumes had ornamented the dead Viking's helmet more than eight centuries ago, the metallic surfaces of the preserved feathers were still brilliant.) At one time, too, the long train feathers were woven into cloth, the warp being of silk and the woof of feathers. The fabric was then fashioned into resplendent robes. To early Christians, the peacock symbolized immortality, and so they adorned churches with the bird's feathers.

Some strange beliefs surround peacocks, their flesh and feathers, in today's world. In Burma and Java, people think that peafowl endanger young children. They are afraid that since the birds like to swallow shiny stones, they may be deceived by the sparkling eyes of children and try to peck them out. Indians, however, like to keep peafowl in their gardens because of the bird's reputation for hypnotic power over serpents. The sight of a mongoose, another foe of snakes, is supposed to have the same effect. The snake does not hide or escape, but steadily gazes at the peacock and before long stretches out on the ground as if dead. Thus, snakes are absent, out of fear or because they are eaten by the birds, from Indian gardens where peafowl roam.

In lands where peafowl are not held sacred, men hunt them as they do game birds like pheasant or partridge in the United States. Many birds are snared in traps, and sometimes hunters race after them on foot and seize them on the run. Peafowl occasionally are tricked into coming close enough to be captured when a man imitates the bird's call from the depths of his chest. People hunt for and eat peafowl eggs too.

On the other hand, Mohammedans in the Malay regions regard the peafowl as unclean and do not eat the bird. It is supposed to have guided the serpent to the Tree of Knowledge in the Garden of Eden and, therefore, is living under an eternal curse.

People of other faiths are not troubled with this notion and willingly eat the flesh. Roast young peacock is delicious, but older birds are incredibly tough. At a grand ball and dinner given by the Iranian consul in New York City in 1974, roast peacock was the main dish along with caviar and other splendid fare. "Peacock tastes like chewy chicken," pronounced one of the honored guests. One might say that peafowl were "saved by the turkey," for once turkeys were discovered in Mexico in the sixteenth century, they gradually turned up on dinner tables in Europe instead of roast peacock. And this native American member of the Phasianidae clan is still popular poultry especially at holiday feasts.

turkey

In the theatrical world there are people who think peacocks bring bad luck, and they speak of the "evil eye" of a peacock plume. In Sinhalese medicine lore, the eye, or ocellus, of the peacock feather is used as an antidote against rat bite. If someone is bitten by a rat on the island of Sri Lanka, formerly Ceylon, he may wrap a feather in a piece of dried plantain leaf and roll it like a cigarette. Then he smokes it, inhaling, three times —once in the morning, once in the evening, and finally on the following morning. By that time the patient should be feeling better.

In the early 1900's, the traffic in peacock skins and feathers was heavy; seventy thousand bundles of eyed plumes were once imported by an English firm in a single week. Nowadays many plumes are still gathered in India and exported widely for use in fashion or home decoration.

Peafowl are by no means an endangered species. Throughout the almost three thousand years that man has known the peacock, it has been prized mainly for its grace and beauty. The peacock survives because among all the pheasants in the wild, there is no more wary bird when threatened, yet none tamer when man domesticates it. When the peacock is kept in captivity, it is prized. A peacock accepts food and shelter, and in return the bird stays fairly close to "home," parades the grounds, and displays its beautiful feathers.

ON DISPLAY

In the East it is often said that peafowl live for a hundred years. Perhaps. In the West, although some zoos keep breeding flocks of peafowl on their grounds for many, many years, the birds are unbanded and at liberty, so they do not have data on how old they are. The London Zoo reports that peafowl of over ten years appear to be rare. (The Zoo does list one at nineteen years.) At the Bronx Zoo, in New York, two Congo peacocks, *Afropavo congensis,* survived for seventeen and twenty-two years respectively. An ornithologist from the San Diego Zoo believes peafowl may live from fifteen to twenty years in temperate climates.

The peafowl colony at large in a beautifully landscaped park, often with brooks or moats and bridges, is among a zoo's most popular sights.

All peafowl are healthier in a semifree environment. The birds do not do well when confined in small places. Peacocks wander freely at some zoos and sometimes stroll out into the streets. The police in Willow Grove, Pennsylvania, recently jailed a peacock when a man driving near his home spied the peacock crossing the street at night. After lodging the bird in a cell, they discovered that it had a Philadelphia Zoo tag around its neck.

Single birds may stray, but pairs generally do not. When new specimens are received at a zoo, they are usually confined in a wire pen for several weeks; then when released, they do not leave the area. Habitually they return to their feeding station and roost on top of the pen in which they have been held. If peafowl stray when first released, one of the pair is returned to the pen in sight of the other. The mate keeps the free bird close by until he is satisfied with his new surroundings.

The common peafowl most often found in zoos are hardy and are kept out of doors all year round. They like a choice of sunlight, outdoor shade, and an open shed facing southward for shelter. Peafowl prefer to roost in fairly high trees on horizontal branches. Several hundred peafowl may congregate at dusk and roost in a group of eucalyptus and acacia trees at a California zoo. Many of the birds perch on branches thirty to forty feet above the ground. Other favored resting spots are fences or perches two to

three inches in diameter, fixed high enough
to keep the male's train clear of the ground.

At liberty, the birds find natural foods such as
insect life, grass, berries, fruits, grains, and
sprouting buds. They also are given additional
food, especially in winter. It may be one of the
high-protein pellet foods used for the feeding of
turkeys, which they gradually become accus-

tomed to. A variety of food is essential so this diet is alternated with grains including corn, wheat, barley, millet, but not oats. Peafowl that eat grain only soon become too fat. They also like dried fruits (large fruits must be cut up), minced, raw, lean meat, hard-boiled eggs, and cooked root vegetables such as carrots, potatoes, and beets. Raw cabbage, lettuce, dandelion, spinach, fresh grass and leaves are provided too. Clean water and grit (sometimes crushed oyster shell) are available at all times.

The birds fare well in family groups at the zoo, especially if weaker peafowl have room enough to avoid the more aggressive individuals. Zoos usually allow the hen to incubate the eggs and rear her own brood, the chicks roaming about with her. If a substitute mother must be used, a quiet turkey hen is most suitable, as their habits are similar. Peachicks have also been raised in brooders.

In general, when peafowl are kept warm and dry and are supplied with a nourishing and varied diet, they are healthy and active. Such birds make beautiful and carefree additions to zoos, parks, and estates. Dampness is bad for peafowl in captivity. Clay soils are not suitable as they retain moisture. Sandy soil is best as it provides perfect drainage and is easily turned up if necessary. Veterinarians have remedies for various illnesses contracted by peafowl. Chicks may contract diphtheria at birth, but it can be prevented and contagion checked in various

ways. There are preventions or cures also for other peafowl ailments, including rickets, colds, coughs, gout, scabies, which attack their legs, and parasitic worms, which cause intestinal upsets.

While raising peafowl has been a hobby enjoyed by royalty and the rich for hundreds of years, keeping ornamental game birds today is an established business and pastime for many of more modest means. On farm and prairie land

and in suburbs outside large cities, these people raise and breed pheasants of different types as well as peafowl. They sell the birds to parks, estates, or bird fanciers, who keep them in outdoor aviaries. They also compete for prizes at shows just as other people do at horse shows or dog shows.

Individual families that like birds can keep hardy common peafowl in outdoor aviaries all year round throughout the country. The wire pen should be as large as possible on well-drained ground, with shade from nearby trees. It should contain fairly high perches, and a roof or shelter is necessary to cover the roosting area in cold and snowy regions. Chopped fresh vegetables and abundant green food must be provided when grass is not accessible to the birds. Their diet includes foods from the kitchen like berries, fruits, chopped raw meat, hard-boiled eggs, bread, and nuts. They also need grains and pellet foods that are available at pet shops, clean water, and suitably sized grit. The birds will unearth worms and insects found in the pen. Their shallow food dishes should be scalded frequently and kept clean.

To one owner of an Indian blue peacock that shares a backyard aviary with five different kinds of pheasants, the birds "are a source of color and

movement and life right outside our dining-room windows. It's a great pleasure to watch them instead of looking at a tree or a piece of statuary and a fountain." The family, who lives on a quarter acre of land, wanted pets that would not require too much care and that they could all enjoy. Their interest was sparked when the father took his ten-year-old son to visit his business partner, who raised and bred pheasants as a hobby.

The father had a greenhouse builder erect the aviary of green-painted steel pipes and green vinyl-coated chicken wire. The eighteen-foot aviary was placed amid a circle of birch trees on a pad of concrete that years ago supported the family pool. Inside stands a cut dead willow tree to provide perches.

The birds feed themselves from a feeder that can hold three weeks' supply of game-bird feed. They drink from a watering device that can be filled with three gallons at a time. A wooden walk about five feet off the ground occupies part of the enclosure. The birds' droppings have no odor, and the aviary needs cleaning only twice a year, when the ground is spaded and disinfected so it does not become "sour."

In 1969, when the family first acquired their new pets, they spent $750 for the aviary, about $75 for the peacock, and $25 each for the different pheasant breeds. After the initial investment, the only cost was a few dollars a week for feed. The peacock, which had the normal ear-splitting call, was medically devoiced, an operation that is performed by animal doctors.

Of course, the landscaped aviary and its colorful inhabitants attract their share of admirers from troops of Girl Scouts and Boy Scouts, classes from the nearby elementary school, experienced bird fanciers, and neighbors of all ages who stroll or bike over "to visit the peacock." A taxi driver from the local railroad station frequently brings people coming to the neighborhood past the house just to point out the birds.

And if the visitors are lucky, perhaps the peacock will make a rattling noise, then suddenly lift and spread its feathered train into a fantastic fan. Maybe it will dance and prance a bit. Then they can see how sparkling and brilliant and magical a peacock really is.

ABOUT THE AUTHOR

Born in Flushing, New York, Lynne Martin was educated in the local schools. Later she worked in public relations and as a freelance writer for newspapers and magazines. Presently she concentrates on writing books for children.

Mrs. Martin's hobbies include indoor and outdoor gardening among many others, and she is especially interested in ecology. She and her husband, a computer systems engineer, live in Roslyn Heights, New York. Their family consists of seven children, three boys and four girls.

ABOUT THE ARTIST

Lydia Rosier was born in Geneva, Switzerland, and received her education in the Netherlands. Later, upon coming to the United States, she studied at the Art Students League and the School of Visual Arts in New York City. In following years she served as art director for William Morrow and has won several top awards and honors in illustration and graphic design. Now she devotes her time to writing and illustrating. She and her husband, also an artist-illustrator, live in New York City.

INDEX

* indicates illustration

aggressive behavior, 23, 32*,
    45*-47
Alexander the Great, 68, 69*
Aristotle, 67
aviary, 88*, 89-92, 90*
Bronx Zoo, 29, 34, 82
Chapin, Dr. James P., 27
chickens, 12*, 13
color, 9, 40
crest, 10*, 11, 29
dance, 11, 47, 93
Darwin, Charles, 38-39
description, 24
digestive system, 56*-57
discovery, 15
diseases, 59, 87*-88
dust bathing, 60*-61
ears, 64-65
enemies, 63*-64*, 76, 77*
fan, display of, 2*, 8*, 9, 11,
    30-34, 31*, 33*, 93*
feathers, 36-41*, 37*, 38*,
    59*, 61

contour, 36, 37*
down, 36, 37*, 51
flight, 36, 37*
    barbs, 36-38, 37*
    barbules, 36-37*
    quill, 36, 37*
    shaft, 36, 37*
    vane, 36, 37*
feeding habits, 20*-21*, 52,
    55*-56, 85-86, 89-90
feet, 24, 56, 62
food, use as, 72-75, 73*, 74*,
    78-80, 79*
history of, 67-78
hybrids, 26-27
India, 18, 19*, 20*, 68, 80,
    81*
keratin, 39
King Solomon, 68
life in captivity, 15, 81, 82-87,
    85*
life-span, 82
London Zoo, 82

melanin, 40
Middle Ages, 68, 72-75, 73*, 74*
migration, 57
molting, 40-41*
myths about, 70-71*, 76, 78, 80
National Zoo, Washington, D.C., 42
native regions, 16*-22, 19*, 20*, 21*, 27
New York Zoological Society, 29
peachicks, 43, 50-53*, 51*, 86
peafowl, 11-12
peahen, 11, 50
Phasianidae, 12*-14*, 13*, 79*
pheasants, 12-14, 13*, 90*, 92
Philadelphia Zoo, 83
Phoenicians, 68
plumes, 9, 30-31*, 36, 63, 75*-76
    eyespot (ocellus), 14*-15, 38*-39, 71*, 80
preening, 58-59*
raising peafowl, 88*-93
reproduction
    breeding, 44, 47, 49
    brood patch, 50
    eggs, 48*, 49-50

incubation, 50
mating ritual, 2*, 32, 46*, 47-49
roosting, 34, 35*, 54, 58, 65-66*, 84-85*
San Diego Zoo, 82
size, 24
species
    Indian blue, 16, 18-21*, 20*, 34, 35*, 90
    white, 25*-26
    pied, 26
    black-winged (black-shouldered), 26, 27*
    Javan green, 16, 22*-24
    Congo (African), 27-29, 28*, 82
strutting, 32-33*
tail, 9-11, 30-31*
temperature, body, 61-62
territory, 45
trade in, 40, 70, 80, 81*
train, 14*, 30-34*, 31*, 33*, 47, 53, 71*
turkey, 79*
Vikings, 75*
Vitellius, 72
voice, 23-24, 29, 42-45, 43*, 66